Leisure Arts 33

Painting
Waterscapes in
Acrylics

Ray Campbell Smith

SEARCH PRESS

Introduction:
Painting materials

Acrylics

Acrylics paints are a modern medium and were not in general use until the early 1960s; yet their sales now rival those of oil paints. What, then, are the special qualities that have made acrylics so popular?

To begin with they may be mixed with water and applied in washes, or they may be used straight from the tube and applied like oil paint. Brushes may be washed under the tap, though this should be done very thoroughly to prevent damage by clogging. Although acrylics may be used to resemble either watercolour or oil, to my mind they are at their best when used in their own right rather than in imitation of another medium.

Acrylics are versatile and may be used on almost any grease-free or dust-free surface, including hardboard (masonite), paper and canvas. When dry they form a rubbery film which is impervious to water and so colour cannot be lifted out with a damp brush as it can with watercolour. This film is very tough, adheres well and is resistant to fading. Unlike watercolour, which becomes lighter in tone on drying, acrylics become appreciably darker, and due allowance needs to be made for this.

The quick-drying property of acrylics has one disadvantage which soon becomes apparent when one is working in the open, particularly if the weather is sunny and hot. They can dry *too* quickly, both on one's support and on one's mixing palette, and it is all too easy for particles of dry paint to get in the way. But there is a remedy: if one uses a retarder, the paint remains workable for much longer. I also use a small spray in such conditions and periodically give my mixing palette a quick squirt with it.

There are various other media available for specific purposes: gel medium for impasto work, a gloss and a matt medium for increasing flow and transparency, and a gloss and matt varnish. Experiment will show you which, if any, of the aids will help your work. Now I only use the varnish, and find that a mixture of matt and gloss gives an attractive satiny finish.

Brushes

You will need a range of hog-hair brushes, the size and shape depending upon the scale and style of your work. I use a mixture of flats, rounds and filberts in a wide variety of sizes, plus a couple of small sables for detail work. You will also need a palette knife for mixing the paint and cleaning your palette after use, and, perhaps, a painting knife if you wish to experiment with that style of painting. Painting-knife work can be attractive, though it demands a generous amount of paint to be effective and in the early stages this can prove expensive.

Palettes

Wooden or plastic palettes are normally used for acrylic painting but almost any smooth, impervious surface will do. In the studio I use a panel of chipboard, faced on either side with white Formica (cadged from the contractor who modernised our kitchen) and very useful it is.

Technique

As with oil painting, I first give my support a dilute overall wash of some warm colour suitable for the subject, often a mixture of raw or burnt sienna. This kills the rather inhibiting white of canvas or paper and, if allowed to show through later work, helps to unify the painting and hold it together. I then block in the larger areas of light and shade. When working in the open it is advisable to establish the shadows early on and then stick to them whatever the sun may do in the meantime. The shaded areas should be deeper in tone than the shadows they represent, to allow for the subsequent addition of lighter-toned paint to create texture – as in oils, working from dark to light. I sometimes find it helpful to use full washes of paint for large smooth areas such as a sky or sheets of water, as these contrast well with the rougher, broken applications of paint to adjacent areas.

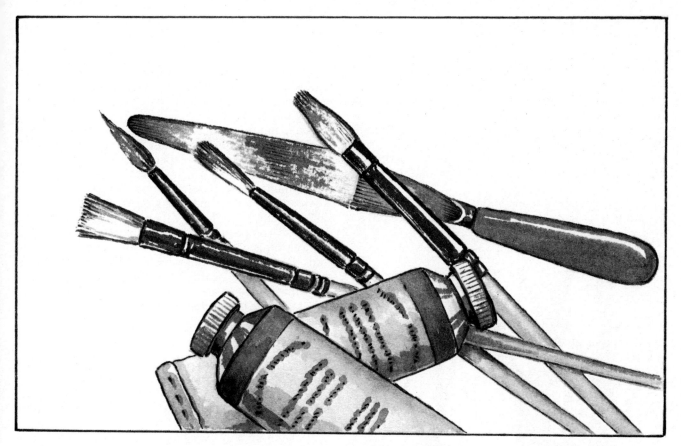

Acrylic tubes, hog-hair brushes (from left to right – flat, round, filbert), sable brush, palette knife.

It is good practice to stick to a limited palette as this tends to give one's work a unity which the employment of a wide range of colours can easily destroy. It also makes it easier to get to know the individual properties of the chosen tubes more thoroughly, though this aspect is perhaps less important than it is with watercolour where the handling characteristics of different colours can differ considerably.

Finally, it pays to work quickly and boldly, not only to avoid the problem of premature drying, but because it can impart looseness and spontaneity to one's work – this in the comforting knowledge that mistakes can be readily rectified without loss of freshness.

Water as a subject

In this book I shall be dealing with water in its natural forms – seas, lakes, rivers, streams, ponds, waterfalls, rapids, puddles, even wet roads. I shall cover both still water and moving water, and will examine how this colourless liquid can borrow colour from its surroundings. It is a difficult but rewarding subject, and one that has attracted artists throughout the ages. To quote but one example, Turner's fascination with water is apparent in many of his finest works.

One occasionally sees paintings which have for their subject just sea and sky, and very compelling they can be in the hands of a master. However I am more concerned with water as part of the landscape, including its natural surroundings – the banks of inland water and the shores of sea and ocean.

Water not only forms an integral part of the natural world, but its presence adds an extra dimension to the landscape. It can impart a sparkle to an otherwise drab scene as, for example, when a pale sky is reflected in the rain - puddled ruts of a farm track (see opposite), or when a shining river meanders across the dun-coloured saltings to the sea. The very flatness of still water can be an aid to composition, contrasting as it does with the vertical forms of adjacent features such as buildings and trees. Beginners sometimes find it difficult, however, to make the surface of their water appear to lie flat and they unwittingly create the impression that it is flowing uphill. This is due to faulty perspective in drawing the margin between land and water (see page 10-11).

Still water

Perfectly still expanses of water give rise to perfect mirror images. While these have an undoubted appeal of their own, for the painter this attraction has it dangers. Unless the scene depicted is a very simple one, the mass of inverted detail in the reflection can make for an over-elaborate and over-busy foreground. However, a gentle breeze, blowing across the surface of the water, breaks up these reflections and creates a softer effect which does not compete with the detail above it. This softer treatment of reflections is certainly a simpler matter than attempting mirror images which present

Tree group reflections.

There is not much water in this painting, but the puddles in the ruts play the vital role of linking the luminous sky to the dark landscape and help to heighten the dramatic contrast.

tricky problems of perspective to the inexperienced artist. But even with these more diffuse reflections it is important to ensure there is harmony between them and the scene above. This may seem self-evident, but it is surprising how many paintings contain reflections which have little in common with the subject-matter above them.

The next step is to analyse the tones of the objects reflected, bearing in mind that light objects have rather darker reflections and dark objects somewhat lighter ones. The colour of the reflections will be modified to some extent by the local colour of the water, and this effect will be the greater the more directly one is looking down into the water.

Draughtsmanship

However good the painting technique, a finished work is only as good as the underlying drawing. This is why we should do all we can to improve our draughtsmanship at every opportunity.

One way to do this is to have a sketchbook always at hand and to use it to record quick impressions of any and every subject that catches our eye. The majority of these sketches will probably never be developed, but the very act of making them gradually improves our technique and makes us more alert to the visual opportunities about us.

Recognising a good subject is a skill that needs nurturing. Some people find that the use of a 'viewfinder' (see below) helps them to spot a promising subject. This aid is nothing more than a piece of stiff card with a rectangular aperture, about the size of a postcard, cut in the middle. It is surprising how this simple device can help to isolate good compositions from a complex scene and, moreover, relate the lines of the chosen subject to the lines which form the margin of the paper or canvas.

Composition and balance

Good composition is not easy to define. If a painting is well composed, of course, there is a balance about it that we find pleasing and satisfying; but it is easier to list the points to avoid. We should, for example, avoid putting a dominant line, such as the horizon, exactly half-way up the paper, or a strong vertical, such as a church spire, midway between the left-hand and right-hand margins. We should also avoid including a road or track that carries our eye straight off the paper and should arrange the picture so that the principal construction lines seem to point towards our centre of interest. Tonal balance is equally important: the tonal weight should not be just on one side of the painting.

Developing a subject

Once we have found a subject that appeals, the next step is to make a series of quick sketches of it from varying viewpoints. One of these will probably turn out to be more pleasing than the others, because it is the most satisfying composition, and this should form the basis of the painting. It will also contain a number of tonal contrasts that will help to give the painting life and character. The sketches (opposite) of an old bridge spanning a slow-moving river were made with this object in view. I finally selected sketch no.4 because it seemed the most balanced composition and the light stone of the bridge stood out boldly against the darker buildings and trees behind it.

The amount of drawing you need to do before starting painting will depend not only on your skill and experience but upon the complexity of your subject. A simple river scene with trees and bushes and not much else will need very little drawing, although it is always wise to establish the lines of the river itself and correct,

at this stage, any tendency for the water to flow uphill. If boats, bridges and buildings are to be included, then more drawing will need to be undertaken. Far better to work out your problem and correct your mistakes on sketching paper than do it on the painting itself.

If for any reason the painting cannot be done on the spot, then the chosen sketch has to contain considerably more information, not only on line, but on tone and colour as well. Tone we can indicate effectively with a pencil, or charcoal, but colours will have to be indicated by means of colour notes. Experienced painters usually evolve their own shorthand to indicate colours and materials – many of my own sketches contain almost as many initials as they do lines.

This painting of a farm pond, bathed in evening sunlight, illustrates some of the points already made. The surface of the water is ruffled by the breeze just sufficiently to break up the mirror image, although the reflections of the main features are still recognisable.

There are a number of places where lights are placed against darks in order to enhance tonal contrast and give the painting more form and interest. Notice also how the line of the middle-distance hedge leads the eye towards the group of farm buildings.

In this painting the breeze has produced ripples on the surface of the lake water. These are particularly noticeable in the reflection of the margin between land and sky and are boldly indicated. As they recede they become foreshortened to the point at which they cannot be painted individually – this is, fortunately, off the paper! Notice how the strip of pale, wind-ruffled water conveniently separates the hills from their reflection, and how tonal contrasts abound.

Reflections and perspective in still water

Although the diffused reflections discussed on pages 4-5 do not necessitate an exact application of the rules of perspective, it is still necessary for the artist to understand the theoretical construction involved in order to avoid errors. If he knows where the mirror image would fall, he is unlikely to offend the laws of perspective too flagrantly when going for softer effects.

To decide how much of an object standing a little way from the water's edge will be reflected, a simple construction is necessary. First, imagine that the horizontal plane of the surface of the water cuts right through the bank to a point vertically below the object in question. This is shown in Figure 1, which demonstrates how much of the church steeple will be reflected. Figure 2 shows a similar construction in the case of a river bridge. In both cases the vertical arrows above and below the horizontal axis line (AA) are of equal length.

If the water in a lake or a river fails to lie flat, it will be due to faulty perspective in the drawing of the banks. Another common fault is that of making the line of a distant margin vary too much in a vertical plane. The distant shoreline of a large lake will appear almost as a straight line, unless one is looking down on the scene from well above water level. At such a distance flat areas are very much foreshortened and however indented the far shoreline, any deviation from a horizontal straight line will be very slight. By virtue of this foreshortening even a sizeable field will appear as a narrow strip.

A sudden breeze, blowing across the surface of an expanse of water, will produce an area of lighter colour which breaks up the smooth reflections around it. This can occur whenever an errant breeze happens to blow and the resultant colour is lighter because wind-ruffled water reflects much more of the sky above. This

Fig 1

Fig 2

Reflections in a wet street.

phenomenon can be put to good use if, for example, we wish to interpose a band of paler colour between land and water for compositional reasons, as in the painting of the lake on page 9. This horizontal stretch of light colour can serve the additional purpose of helping the surface of the water to 'lie flat'.

In dealing with the problem of reflections in still water, we must not forget such shining surfaces as wet roads and pavements. Dry metalled roads are not a very appealing subject for the painter but wet tarmacadam is another matter and offers attractive and interesting possibilities in the reflections. These will be modified to some extent by unevennesses in the surface, or by tyre marks, or gutters, but we must include them, otherwise our wet roads will look somewhat too Venetian!

Stage 1

Stage 2

Stage 3

Stage 4

River painting: demonstration

Size; 228 mm × 305 mm (9 in. × 12 in.)
Paper: Arches Rough 600 gsm (300 lb.).
Brushes: 7, 8, 9 bristle and 6 sable.
Colours: titanium white, Payne's grey, raw sienna, burnt sienna, light red, ultramarine, Winsor blue.

Stages 1–2

With the sable brush and diluted Payne's grey I sketch the principal lines of the composition. Using washes of raw sienna for the sunlit clouds, ultramarine and light red for the cloud shadows, and ultramarine for the patch of blue sky – all blended with titanium white – I paint in the sky, and allow the colours to merge at the margin.

Using ultramarine, a little light red and titanium white I paint in the distant hills. I add the wooded areas with a deeper mix of the same colours. Then I paint in the

Stage 5 – the finished painting

middle distance fields, with a blend of titanium white, Winsor blue and raw sienna.

Stages 3–4

The nearer fields I tackle with a mixture of ultramarine, raw sienna and titanium white. Next I prepare a stiff mix of Winsor blue and raw and burnt sienna, plus a little titanium white, and paint in the trees, using the roughness of the paper to achieve a broken edge. With a

slightly lighter mixture than for the trees I paint in the river banks and apply texturing to the nearer fields.

Stage 5- the finished painting

I prepare liquid washes similar to those used for the sky and apply them to the river area, using bold, vertical strokes. The reflections of the trees and river banks are added through a rather paler version of the mix used for the trees themselves and allowing blending to occur.

Atmosphere

The landscape artist aspires to more than the mere mechanical recording of the outdoor scene and seeks to breathe life and feeling into his subject-matter. He is therefore more concerned with feeling than with accurate detail.

The murky and misty weather conditions which soften outlines and clothe the landscape in mystery require us to be imaginative in recording our impressions of the scene. In this way we encourage those who view our work to use their own imaginations.

The paintings on these two pages both attempt to capture the effects of mist and drizzle on a city scene.

The background in the painting above is largely obscured by the mist and only the vaguest forms of the buildings are suggested. I have emphasized the radiance created in the misty air by the luminous patch of sky on the right of the painting, and have indicated how the reflected light emphasizes the feeling of wetness on road

and pavement. The treatment of the figures, little more than grey silhouettes, reinforces the overall atmosphere of mystery.

Lakeside city

Here the effect of the misty conditions is to convert the distant buildings into a grey silhouette, paler at the base where the mist is rising from the lake. A gentle breeze has ruffled the surface of the water to create a paler stretch which provides a convenient break between the buildings and the lake. The nearer objects – the figures, the trees and the railings – have been painted deeper tones to provide contrast with the paler background and so create a strong feeling of recession.

Conditions such as these encourage me to use subtle, pearly colours instead of varying tones of grey. This greatly enhances the attractiveness of the painting.

Fishing boats

These beamy old wooden hulls, winched up the shingly foreshore and standing out boldly against a stormy sky, made a subject I could not resist. Much as one admires the greyhound lines of modern racing yachts, there is something basic and honest about the solid shapes of working boats.

The sky was cloudy but lively and constantly changing. I chose a moment therefore when a lighter patch appeared immediately behind the boats, to enhance their dramatic impact. To balance the tonal weight of the boats and the foreshore on the right of the painting, I decided to pace the heaviest clouds on the left. This has the additional advantage of providing a telling contrast with the light tone of the sea.

A foreshortened cloud shadow added emphasis to these clouds and gave the expanse of water a feeling of perspective. The wet shingle by the water's edge was comparatively dark in tone and this provided useful additional contrast.

Some painters, with orderly minds, have a way of tidying up the scene before them, but it is a temptation which should be resisted with such scenes as this, for the presence of a certain amount of clutter adds to the atmosphere and the character of the subject. After all, who ever saw a tidy boatyard?

The treatment of the shingle is fairly rough as I did not want to divert attention from the fishing boats or get bogged down with painting individual stones – a quick indication of a few is enough to suggest the remainder.

Water in movement

Moving water represents a more difficult problem than still water, not least because the very movement makes it more difficult to study. The first stage is careful observation; the moving water must then be mentally 'frozen' at a point when its form appears most expressive. Although the subject is always on the move, the chosen instant will constantly recur, not in exactly the same form, perhaps, for no two waves, or two eddies, are identical, but closely enough for practical purposes.

The sea

When tackling seascapes, the first question is, where to place the horizon? As I have pointed out, it should not be exactly half-way up the page, so the basic decision is whether to give greater prominence to the sea or to the sky. If the sky is an interesting one, a low horizon will do it better justice. This will entail adopting a low viewpoint and so condensing the expanse of sea. There is a positive advantage in this for the foreshortening of the wave pattern will force us to concentrate on the nearer waves, to the benefit of the composition. A higher viewpoint will take in many more waves and it is all to easy then for these to become repetitive and produce a 'corrugated iron' effect.

Another early decision to make is whether to paint looking straight out to sea or to adopt a slightly oblique angle. I generally prefer the second alternative as it avoids the danger of the composition degenerating into a series of horizontal lines. If I include a strip of sand at the edge of the sea, for example (see page 23), there may well be a tide-mark of pebbles, seaweed or other flotsam and jetsam. This twists and turns with the configuration of the shore and its inclusion can help to describe the contours of the foreshore and add to the interest.

An angry sea is an impressive sight and one that poses a real challenge to the painter. Not only must he or she capture the form and shape of the waves – they must be

imbued with life and movement. The artist will use plenty of white to represent foam and white horses and he will give bursts of spray a soft edge and try to place them against a dark background to provide contrast.

In the painting on this page the massive wave exploding against the stone groyne throws a column of white foam high in the air. Dramatic tonal contrast has been provided by placing it against a dark mass of storm cloud. The low viewpoint emphasizes the height and

power of the waves and makes it a simple matter to concentrate on just one impressive wave and make a feature of it.

Violently moving water is filled with air bubbles. These have the effect of lightening its tone. In this painting the dark treatment of the groyne and the wet sand serves to highlight the pale tone of the sea. The gulls add a crisp note against the lowering sky, and, though small, help to provide compositional balance.

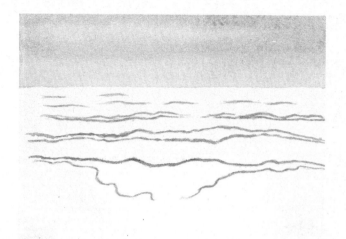

Stage 1

Stage 2

Stage 3

Stage 4

Breaking wave: demonstration

Size; 164 × 228 mm (6½ × 9 in).
Paper: Saunders Not 600 gsm (300 lb).
Brushes: 6, 8, 10 sable.
Colours: titanium white, Payne's grey, raw sienna, light red, ultramarine.

Stage 1

With a dilute wash of Payne's grey, I sketch in the principal lines of the nearer waves and the horizon. As this subject lends itself to a liquid use of acrylics, I choose sable rather than bristle brushes, and use plenty of water. I paint the sky with a wash of raw sienna and a touch of light red and, while this is still wet, apply horizontal strokes of ultramarine and light red to suggest the clouds.

Stage 5 – the finished painting

Stage 2

The near wave is painted with a mixture of raw sienna and Payne's grey; the white paper is left to stand for the foam patterns. I add Payne's grey for the shadowed area at the top of the wave and soften this with clean water to indicate spray.

Stages 3–4

Here I complete the near wave, and indicate the curling line of the second wave with Payne's grey.

Again I complete the distant area of sea with Payne's grey plus a little ultramarine; and I leave chips of white to stand for the white horses.

Stage 5–the finished painting

All that remains now is for me to add some pale shading to the areas of foam in shadow with a mixture of ultramarine, light red and titanium white.

The shoreline

In studying natural water in all its forms, it is necessary to include its setting – the banks of rivers and lakes and the shorelines of seas and oceans. Here I am looking at the foreshore and deciding how best to convey its essence in paint.

On a typical sandy shore, with an ebbing tide, there are three main elements, the sea itself, a strip of wet sand which the sea has left behind, and, below that, a stretch of dry sand.

The sea may, in its turn, be divided into four elements: the dominant form of the nearest line of waves which provides a telling accent; below it the flat foamy expanse of the last spent wave; then the foreshortened area of the more distant waves which will be treated in much less detail; and, perhaps, a distant stretch of cloud shadow which may well extend to the horizon. All these are related, so they must be looked at as a whole and their tone and colour analysed.

The painting on page 23 contains all these elements. The lively, cloudy sky suggests a low horizon. The curving line of the nearest wave is strongly marked while the more distant waves are merely suggested. The strip of wet sand reflects the dark sky above but its deep tone is relieved by lines of foam left by a receding wave. The stretch of dry sand is lighter in tone and this, in turn, is relieved by a dark line of seaweed, roughly parallel to the margin of the sea. The figure and the dog provide a crisp note and are painted dark against light, and light against dark.

Boats are inseparable from the coastal scene and their inclusion adds interest to any marine painting. Their masts can help to 'tie together' the mainly horizontal lines of the typical seascape. In the sketch of the two beached boats on page 22, the masts span the bands of sky, sea and sand and link them together.

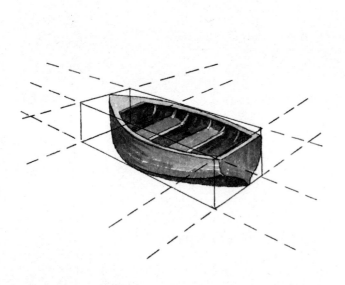

Sea, sky and sand.

Except when drawn in profile boats are tricky subjects and, incorrectly drawn, can look remarkably unsea-worthy. Some teachers suggest using a rectangular framework, with carefully constructed perspective, and drawing the boat shape within it, as in the left-hand sketch opposite. While this is some check against gross error, only careful observation will reveal the subtle line of the keel and gunwale.

Stage 1

Stage 2

Stage 3

Stage 4

Painting sailing barges: demonstration

Size: 180 mm × 255 mm (7in. × 10in.)
Paper: Arches Rough 600 gsm (300 lb.)
Brushes: nos. 7, 8, 9 bristle, and no. 6 sable.
Colours: titanium white, Payne's grey, raw sienna, burnt sienna, light red, ultramarine.

Stage 1
I tint the whole of the paper with a wash of raw and burnt sienna. With the sable brush and dilute Payne's grey I then sketch in the outlines of the sailing barges.

Stage 2
Mixes of raw sienna are prepared with a little light red for the sunlit clouds, ultramarine and light red for the cloud shadows, and ultramarine and Payne's grey for the blue sky – all blended with titanium white. Then I paint

Stage 5 – the finished painting

in the sky and the misty line of cloud shadow on the horizon.

Stages 3–4
The sea is painted with titanium white, Payne's grey and raw sienna, with a hint of warmth added here and there with light red. The more distant sailing barge is rendered very simply with light red, ultramarine and titanium white.

I put in the suggestion of soft wave shadows on the sea and paint in, a little more crisply, the moored barge, adding detail with the tip of the sable brush.

Stage 5 – the finished painting
All that remains now is to paint in the reflections against the luminous evening sky which shades into the limpid water below.

Movement in fresh water

In the painting, on page 27, of a swiftly flowing, shallow stream, my main objective was to capture the feeling of movement in the water. As I felt this could best be achieved by a bold and loose approach, I used plenty of white to represent the water foaming past the rocks and also to indicate the light catching the crest of the ripples.

The effect of the strong current was to produce longitudinal patterns in the water and these I have simplified. Most of the movement was in the centre and towards the nearer bank, while the rather smooth water close to the far bank naturally reflected more of the deeper tones above it. The dark forms of the nearer tree

Mountain tarn.

26

Fast flowing stream.

trunks, against the lighter area beyond, not only provided useful contrast, but assisted in the tonal balance of the painting.

In the painting of the mountain tarn (page 26), movement is confined to the area of wind-ruffled water below the far bank, and to the nearer ripples caused by the small beck entering on the right. Wind-ruffled water reflects, of course, the sky overhead rather than what lies beyond, and it is always lighter in tone than smooth water. Here it is shown as a narrow, horizontal strip of white. The ripples caused by the entry of the little mountain stream have been simplified and put in boldly. Both these modifications to the smooth surface assist the perspective of the tarn and help its waters to lie flat.

Painting a waterfall: demonstration

Size: 222 mm × 222 mm (9¼ in × 9¼ in.).
Paper: Fine grain canvas board.
Brushes: nos. 7, 8 and 9 bristle.
Colours: titanium white, Payne's grey, raw sienna, burnt sienna, light red, ultramarine.

I wanted to record the smooth arcs of the water as it swept over successive drops. I also hoped to capture the light tones of the spray against the darker rocks and the dappled sunlight against the deeper forms of the trees.

Stage 1

I give the canvas an overall wash of raw and burnt sienna, and allow small chips of this warm tone to persist into the finished painting. Next I sketch in the main construction lines of the composition with dilute Payne's grey.

Stage 2

I block in the rock formations with a deep mixture of ultramarine, burnt sienna and a spot of titanium white. Then I add a little more ultramarine and white to the same mix and paint in the area of shadow behind the tree trunks.

With varying mixtures of grey/green and brown (respectively Payne's grey, raw sienna, white and burnt sienna with a touch of ultramarine), I next paint in roughly the shadowed areas of grass, and apply the same grey/green to the smooth curve of the water and a little Payne's grey and white to the shadowed areas of spray.

Stage 3–the finished painting

At this point my object must be to add lighter tones to some of the darker areas, to bring them to life, using Payne's grey, light red and white on the rocks; also in order to indicate algae and moss on tree trunks and rocks, I use a mixture of Payne's grey, raw sienna and white. Next I paint the sun-dappled forest floor with raw sienna, a little Payne's grey and white, and finally put in the highlights on the water and the spray with titanium white and a very little Payne's grey.

Stage 3 – the finished painting

29

Fountains

Man has long recognised the decorative properties of water and has used it to improve the appearance of his environment. The great landscape gardeners of the eighteenth and early nineteenth centuries used to dam up streams to create artificial lakes, to construct waterfalls, and build ornamental fountains for their noble patrons. Those entrusted with the improvement of towns and cities also recognised the possibilities of moving water and today many cities of the world possess fine fountains, often combined with statuary, to enhance and dignify their centres.

In the painting of the park fountain, the jets of water, lit by a strong lateral sun, are placed against a dark background of foliage to create lively tonal contrast. The vertical form of the fountain is echoed in the repeated verticals of the tree trunks and balanced by the strong

horizontals of the tree shadows. These shadows also provide useful counterchange with the light-coloured pond surround.

Though the general treatment is lighter, a similar approach is adopted in the city centre painting, with the jets of water placed against the grey mass of the tall buildings. The equestrian statue and the figures on the left help to balance the dominant form of the fountain.

Page 32. Sailing barge at anchor. There are not many of these fine old craft left. They are no longer used as coastal bulk carriers but serve social and recreational purposes.

With their solid, beamy hulls, the rich red-browns of their sails and the bold verticals and diagonals of their masts, spars and rigging, they make splendid subjects. I painted this group on a day calm enough to produce interesting reflections and sought to emphasise the dark impact of the furled sails and masts against a bright sky, using ultramarine, light red, raw sienna, burnt sienna and, of course, titanium white. (Original size: 172 mm × 221 mm/ 6.8in. × 8.3in.)

Acknowledgements

PAINTING WATERSCAPES IN ACRYLICS

Text, drawings and paintings by
Ray Campbell Smith

Text, illustrations, arrangement and typography
copyright © Search Press Limited 1988

This volume first published in Great Britain 1988
by Search Press Ltd, Wellwood, North Farm
Road, Tunbridge Wells, Kent TN2 3DR

U.S. Artists Materials Trade Distributor:
Winsor & Newton, Inc.
P.O. Box 1519 Winsor Drive, Secaucus,
NJ 07094

Canadian Distributor:
Anthes Universal Limited,
341 Heart Lake Road South, Brampton, Ontario
L6W 3K8

ISBN 0 85532 624 7

Typeset by Scribe Design, Gillingham, Kent
Made and printed in Spain by
Salingraf S.A.L., Bilbao